The Selfless Way of Christ
Downward Mobility and the Spiritual Life

The Selfless Way of Christ
Downward Mobility and the Spiritual Life

HENRI NOUWEN
With Illustrations by Vincent van Gogh

DARTON·LONGMAN+TODD

Grateful acknowledgment is made to *Sojourners* magazine, in which this book was originally serialized in 1981.

Published in 2007 by Orbis Books, Maryknoll, NY 10545-0308.

Published in Great Britain in 2007 by Darton, Longman and Todd Ltd, 1 Spencer Court, 140-142 Wandsworth High Street, London SW18 4JJ.

Reprinted 2011, 2013, 2016, 2018

For more information about Henri Nouwen, his work, and the work of the Henri Nouwen Society, visit www.HenriNouwen.org.

A catalogue record for this book is available from the British Library.

ISBN-13: 978-0-232-52707-0

Printed and bound in Great Britain by
Bell and Bain Ltd, Glasgow.

CONTENTS

FOREWORD

One of the earliest Christian hymns describes the humility of Christ, who, though "his state was divine," did not cling to his equality with God "but emptied himself to assume the condition of a slave" (Phil 2:6–8). Even at the dawn of the church this voluntary self-emptying of power, status, and security offered a powerfully counter-cultural statement. It set the way of Christ in bold contrast to the values of Empire, and thus set a challenge to all Christ's followers.

This "selfless way of Christ" is the theme in this short work, one of a number of books that Henri Nouwen wrote in his years as a professor at Yale Divinity School. It was serialized in 1981 in *Sojourners,* a journal whose blend of evangelical witness and social commitment resonated well with Nouwen's themes. Nouwen also explored its publication with an English editor, who urged him to expand his reflections with more concrete examples from Christian literature and actual life. But for whatever reason, the book was never published.

In some ways Nouwen was responding to a particular time. The prosperity of the early 1980s had given rise to a new phenomenon: the "Yuppy"—short for "young, upwardly-mobile professional." This yuppy class set the tastes and defined the values for much of the culture—values, as Nouwen recognized, that ran utterly contrary to the spirit of the Gospel. More than a simple craving for pleasure and material possessions, "yuppy values" bought into the same temptations presented to Christ in the wilderness: to be "powerful, relevant, and spectacular." To these temptations, as Nouwen recognized, Christians, even those engaged in professional ministry or seminary education, were just as susceptible.

But for Nouwen, too, these temptations struck close to home. As a professor at an Ivy League school and as a much-celebrated spiritual writer, Nouwen wrestled personally with the meaning of his own vocation, and the question of where God was calling him. Though he tried to maintain a simple life, rooted in prayer and obedience to the disciplines of "the church, the Book, and the heart," still he suffered doubts about his own middle-class life, his comfortable status as a professor, and his enjoyment of "human applause." Was God calling him to let go of all these things for the sake of a deeper faithfulness?

Reading these chapters today, especially in light of Nouwen's later writing, one is struck by a rather harsh and penitential tone—an emphasis on selflessness and sacrifice that overshadows any sense of the joy and celebration that are also available on the way of discipleship. But in some ways Nouwen was writing to himself—struggling with his own restless heart, his own tendency to cling to a false and "needy" self. He was describing his own compulsion "to be seen, praised, and admired." That struggle would continue, even after his sojourn among the poor of Latin America, his forays into the monastic world of a Trappist monastery, and his acceptance of a professorship at Harvard Divinity School. It would continue until the end of his life.

But a turning point came in 1986 when he accepted a call to serve as pastor to a L'Arche community in Toronto. There, for the last ten years of his life, he lived in community among adults with intellectual disabilities, adults who knew nothing of his famous books or his reputation as a speaker.

It was an experience of true "downward mobility," an experience in which he truly entered into the "selfless way of Christ." Many of the same themes appeared in his later books, but now with a new concrete reference and a new authenticity. Above all, his insights were leavened by his discovery of what it means to be "beloved of God."

More than a decade after Nouwen's death, his words continue to challenge and enlighten. They still serve to shake us loose from the values of a world obsessed with image, power, and prestige—not for the sake of grim "self-denial," but so that we might discover, as Nouwen increasingly did, the joy and freedom of our true life in Christ.

Robert Ellsberg

Introduction

Something which existed since the beginning,
that we have heard
and we have seen with our own eyes;
that we have watched
and touched with our hands;
the Word, who is life—
this is our subject.

— 1 JOHN 1:1

More clearly than any other text in the New Testament, this passage shows that our vocation of Christian ministry emerges from an experience involving our whole being. The subject of our ministry is Jesus Christ, the Word who was from the beginning with God and was made flesh to live among us (cf. John 1:1–14). To be a Christian is to witness to this Word, to reveal the presence of this Word within us as well as among us. Yet this witness, which takes the form of preaching and teaching, of celebrating and counseling, of organizing and struggling to alleviate the suffering of our fellow human beings, is a true witness only when it emerges from a genuine personal encounter, a true experience of love. We can only call ourselves witnesses of Jesus when we have heard him with our own ears, seen him with our own eyes, and touched him with our own hands.

The basis of the mission of the twelve apostles was not their knowledge, training, or character, but their having lived with Jesus. Paul, who was not with Jesus while he was traveling with his disciples, encountered him on the road to Damascus. This experience was the foundation on which all his apostolic work was built.

There has never been a Christian witness whose influence has not been directly related to a personal and intimate experience of the Lord. This deep and personal encounter can take as many forms and shapes as there are people, cultures, and ages. Ignatius of Antioch, Anthony of the Desert, Gregory the Great, Benedict, Bernard, and Francis, Ignatius of Loyola, Teresa of Avila, John of the Cross, Martin Luther, John Wesley, George Fox, and John Bunyan, Charles de Foucauld, Dag Hammarskjold, Martin Luther King, Jr., Thomas Merton, Jean Vanier, Mother Teresa, Dorothy Day—all these witnesses have seen the Lord, and their actions and words emerge from that vision.

Thus, ministry and the spiritual life belong together. Living a spiritual life is living in an intimate communion with the Lord. It is seeing, hearing, and touching. Living a life of ministry is witnessing to him in the midst of this world. It is opening the eyes of our brothers and sisters in the human family to his presence among us, so that they too may enter into this relationship of love.

When our ministry does not emerge from a personal encounter, it quickly becomes a tiring routine and a boring job. On the other hand, when our spiritual life no longer leads to an active ministry, it quickly degenerates into introspection and self-scrutiny, and thus loses its dynamism. Our life in Christ and our ministry in his name belong together as the two beams of the cross.

This direct relationship between our vocation to ministry and our spiritual life is the theme of this book.

I.

Downward Mobility as Christian Vocation

In one of the most profound prayers ever written, the apostle Paul writes to the Christians of Ephesus:

May the God of our Lord Jesus Christ, the Father of glory, give you a spirit of wisdom and perception of what is revealed, to bring you to full knowledge of God. May God enlighten the eyes of your mind so that you can see what hope God's call holds for you, what rich glories God has promised the saints will inherit and how infinitely great is the power that God has exercised for us believers. This you can tell from the strength of God's power at work in Christ when God used it to raise him from the dead and to make him sit at God's right hand, in heaven.

— EPHESIANS 1:17–20

This prayer makes clear that the spiritual life is a life guided by the same Spirit who guided Jesus Christ. The Spirit is the breath of Christ in us, the divine power of Christ active in us, the mysterious source of new vitality by which we are made aware that it is not we who live, but Christ who lives in us (cf. Galatians 2:20). Indeed, to live a spiritual life means to become living Christs. It is not enough to try to imitate Christ as much as possible; it is not enough to remind others of Jesus; it is not even enough to be inspired by the words and actions of Jesus Christ. No, the spiritual life presents us with a far more radical demand: to be living Christs here and now, in time and history.

We will never come to know our true vocation in life unless we are willing to grapple with the radical claim the gospel places on us. During the past twenty centuries many Christians have heard this radical call and have responded to it in true obedience. Some became hermits in the desert, while others became servants in the city. Some went to distant lands as preachers, teachers, and healers, while others remained where they were, raised families, and worked faithfully. Some became famous, while others remained unknown. Although their responses reveal an extraordinary diversity, these Christians all heard the call to follow Christ without compromise.

Regardless of the particular shape we give to our lives, Jesus' call to discipleship is primal, all-encompassing, all-inclusive, demanding a total commitment. One cannot be a little bit for Christ, give him some attention, or make him one of many concerns.

Is it possible to follow Christ while fulfilling the demands of the world, to listen to Christ while paying equal attention to others, to carry Christ's cross while carrying many other burdens as well? Jesus certainly appears to draw a very sharp distinction. "No one can be the slave of two masters" (Matthew 6:24), he insisted, and he did not hesitate to confront us with the uncompromising demands of his call: "It is a narrow gate and hard road that leads to life . . . Anyone who prefers father or mother to me is not worthy of me" (Matthew 7:14, 10:37).

These challenging words are not meant only for a few of Jesus' followers who have a so-called "special vocation." Rather, they are for all who consider themselves Christians. They indicate the radical nature of the call. There is no easy way to follow Christ. As he himself says, "Whoever is not for me is against me" (Matthew 12:30).

Upward Mobility

O^{ur} lives in this technological and highly competitive society are characterized by a pervasive drive for upward mobility. It is difficult for us even to imagine ourselves outside of this upwardly mobile lifestyle. Our whole way of living is structured around climbing the ladder of success and making it to the top. Our very sense of vitality is dependent upon being part of the upward pull and upon the joy provided by the rewards given on the way up.

Our parents, teachers, and friends impress upon us from the moment we are able to pick up the cues that it is our holy task to make it in this world. To be a real man or woman is to show that one cannot only survive the long competitive struggle for success but also come out victorious.

Individuals as well as institutions tell us in a variety of ways that we must conquer knowledge and people; we must strive to wield influence and be successful. And even love itself is either something to be conquered or a reward for the victorious.

Thus, life is presented as a series of battles which we can win or lose. When we win we have lived up to the ideals of our milieu, but when we lose it is clearly because of our own shortcomings.

In an impressive book, *The Hidden Injuries of Class,* authors Jonathan Cobb and Richard Sennett make it clear that we are trained to believe, even with the most blatant evidence to the contrary, that there is no one but ourselves to blame for our failures. If we remain uneducated, poor, or unemployed, if we have an unhappy marriage or uncooperative children, the main reason is that we have simply not tried hard enough. We

have been lazy, undisciplined, immoral, or just stupid. As a result of hearing this message, our society is filled with people who suffer not only from unemployment or a broken family but also from guilt and shame.

I am not denigrating ambition, nor am I against progress and success. But true growth is something other than the uncontrolled drive for upward mobility in which making it to the top becomes its own goal and in which ambition no longer serves a wider ideal. There is a profound difference between the false ambition for power and the true ambition to love and serve. It is the difference between trying to raise ourselves up and trying to lift up our fellow human beings.

The problem is not in the desire for development and progress as an individual or a community, but in making upward mobility itself into a religion. In this religion we believe that success means that God is with us while failure means that we have sinned. The question then is, "Is God running with us?" If so, then God will make us win.

We are taught to conceive of development in terms of an ongoing increase in human potential. Growing up means becoming healthier, stronger, more intelligent, more mature, and more productive. Consequently we hide those who do not affirm this myth of progress, such as the elderly, prisoners, and those with mental disabilities. In our society, we consider the upward move the obvious one while treating the poor cases who cannot keep up as sad misfits, people who have deviated from the normal line of progress.

When we look on the national level, we see the blatant and shocking implications of the idolatry of upward mobility. We are so dedicated to the goal of ever-increasing growth and develop-

ment that we cannot imagine anyone being elect-
ed to public office without promising to increase
the nation's wealth and power. Those who advance
an agenda based on different values effectively
exclude themselves from national leadership. If
anything is certain, it is that this nation desires to
be the best, the strongest, and the most powerful.
The attitude of "We're number one!" is nurtured
with all diligence and on all levels: in athletics,
business, technology, and military power.

Moreover, we expect more of the things we
have, whether that be bronze, silver, or gold
medals; computers, satellites, or laboratories;
nuclear warheads, missiles, or submarines. It is this
drive for more that has brought us to the brink of
a war that cannot be won.

Downward Mobility

The story of our salvation stands radically over and against the philosophy of upward mobility. The great paradox which Scripture reveals to us is that real and total freedom is only found through downward mobility. The Word of God came down to us and lived among us as a slave. The divine way is indeed the downward way.

In the center of our faith as Christians stands the mystery that God chose to reveal the divine mystery by unreserved submission to the downward pull. God not only chose an insignificant people to carry the Word of salvation through the centuries, not only chose a small remnant of those people to fulfill God's promises, not only chose a humble girl in an unknown town in Galilee to become the temple of the Word, but God also chose to manifest the fullness of divine love in a man whose life led to a humiliating death outside the walls of the city.

This mystery was so deeply ingrained in the minds and hearts of the early Christians that they sang in the hymn of Christ:

> *His state was divine*
> *yet he did not cling*
> *to his equality with God*
> *but emptied himself*
> *to assume the condition of a slave*
> *and become as we are;*
> *and being as we are,*
> *he was humbler yet,*
> *even to accepting death,*
> *death on a cross.*
>
> —PHILIPPIANS 2:6–8

Indeed, the one who was from the beginning with God and who was God revealed himself as a small, helpless child; as a refugee in Egypt; as an obedient adolescent and inconspicuous adult; as a penitent disciple of the Baptizer; as a preacher from Galilee, followed by some simple fishermen; as a man who ate with sinners and talked with strangers; as an outcast, a criminal, a threat to his people. He moved from power to powerlessness, from greatness to smallness, from success to failure, from strength to weakness, from glory to ignominy. The whole life of Jesus of Nazareth was a life in which all upward mobility was resisted.

Some people wanted to make him king. They wanted him to show power. They wanted to share in his influence and sit on thrones with him. But he consistently said "no" to all these desires and pointed to the downward way. "The Son of Man has to suffer . . . can you drink the cup?" Even after his death, when his followers spoke of him as a defeated freedom fighter and said, "Our own hope had been that he would be the one to set Israel free" (Luke 24:21), he had to remind them again of the downward way: "Was it not ordained that the Christ should suffer and so enter into his glory?" (Luke 24:26).

Jesus leaves little doubt that the way he lived is the way he offers to his followers: "The disciple is not superior to his teacher, nor the slave to his master" (Matthew 10:24). With great persistence he points out the downward way: "Anyone who wants to be great among you must be your servant, just as the Son of Man came not to be served but to serve" (Matthew 20:26–28). The downward way is the way of the cross: "Anyone who does not take his cross and follow in my footsteps is not worthy of me. Anyone who finds his life will lose it; anyone who

loses his life for my sake will find it" (Matthew 10:39).

The disciple is the one who follows Jesus on his downward path and thus enters with him into new life. The gospel radically subverts the presuppositions of our upwardly mobile society. It is a jarring and unsettling challenge.

Yet, when we have carefully looked into the eyes of the poor, the oppressed, and the lowly, when we have paid humble attention to their ways of living, and when we have listened gently to their observations and perceptions, we might have already a glimpse of the truth Jesus spoke about. It is a glimpse of the "grace-healed eyes" of which Tertullian spoke.

Somewhere deep in our hearts we already know that success, fame, influence, power, and money do not give us the inner joy and peace we crave. Somewhere we can even sense a certain envy of those who have shed all false ambitions and found a deeper fulfillment in their relationship with God. Yes, somewhere we can even get a taste of that mysterious joy in the smile of those who have nothing to lose.

Then we begin to perceive that the downward road is not the road to hell, but the road to heaven. Keeping this in mind can help us accept the fact that in the Reign of God the poor are the messengers of the good news.

These intuitions and insights reveal that something in us is already suspicious about the upward way. But still the radical response of Jesus remains shocking. We are quite willing to say that we should not forget the poor, that we should share our gifts with those less fortunate, and that we should give up some of our surplus for the many who have not made it.

But are we ready to confess that those whom

we should not forget, those who are less fortunate, those who did not make it, are in fact the blessed ones in the Reign of God, the ones who call us to downward mobility as Jesus did? It can all sound rather morbid and depressing, until we come to know that following Jesus on the downward road means entering into a new life, the life of the Spirit of Jesus himself.

The Spiritual Life

If discipleship requires following Jesus in downward mobility, is this truly a human option? Is it possible to take Jesus totally seriously? Or would that simply mean embarking on a self-destructive, even masochistic, road? I wonder if in practice we haven't already answered this question. Haven't we already decided that Jesus cannot be taken at his

word, but rather needs to be adapted to our way of upward mobility?

I am not asking this as a cynic or a moralist. That would not be taking the matter seriously. Rather, I want to raise the question in the context of the spiritual life. If we think that living the downward way is easily within our reach and that our task is simply to imitate Christ, we have misunderstood the basic truth which has been revealed to us.

The downward way is God's way, not ours. God is revealed as God to us in the downward pull, because only the One who is God can be emptied of divine privileges and become as we are. The great mystery upon which our faith rests is that the One who is in no way like us, who cannot be compared with us, nor enter into competition with us, has come among us and taken on our mortal flesh.

This expression of downward mobility is unnatural for us, because it belongs to the essence of our sinful, broken condition that every fiber of our being is infused with the spirit of rivalry and competition. We are always finding ourselves, even against our own best desires and judgments, on the familiar road of upward mobility. The moment we think we are humble, we find ourselves wondering if we are humbler than our neighbor, and looking around to claim our reward.

Downward mobility is the divine way, the way of the cross, the way of Christ. It is precisely this divine way of living that our Lord wants to give to us through his Spirit. How the way of the Spirit differs radically from the way of the world is made clear in the words of the apostle Paul to the Christians of Corinth:

The hidden wisdom of God . . . is the wisdom that none of the masters of this age has ever known . . . We teach . . . the things that no eye has seen and no ear has heard, things beyond the human mind . . . These are the very things that God has revealed to us through the Spirit, for the Spirit reaches the depths of everything, the depths of God . . . Now instead of the spirit of the world, we have received the Spirit that comes from God, to teach us to understand the gifts that God has given us. Therefore we teach . . . in the way the Spirit teaches us; we teach spiritual things spiritually.

—1 CORINTHIANS 2:7–13

These words summarize succinctly the meaning of the spiritual life. They tell us that it is the life in which the Spirit of Christ, who reaches the depths of God, is given to us so that we may know, with a new knowledge of mind and heart, the way of God.

When Jesus died on the cross, the disciples experienced a deep sense of loss and failure. They thought it was all over and clung to each other in the fear that they would be dealt with as Jesus had been. They had not understood the downward way of God. But when, on the day of Pentecost, the Spirit whom Jesus had promised came, everything changed. The Spirit blew their fears away. The Spirit made them see who Jesus truly was, and revealed to them the new way. The Spirit gave them the strength to proclaim to all nations the way of the cross, the downward way, as the way to salvation.

Jesus himself tells us who the Spirit is. On the evening before his death he said to his disciples:

It is for your own good that I am going, because unless I go, the Advocate [the Spirit] will not come to you; but if I do go, I will send it to you . . . And he will lead you

*to the complete truth, since he will not be speaking as
from himself but will only say what he has learned . . .
all he tells you will be taken from what is mine.
Everything the Father has is mine; that is why I said,
"All he tells you will be taken from what is mine."*

—JOHN 16:7–15

Here Jesus reveals to us that the Spirit is the
fullness of God's being. It is the fullness that Jesus
calls "the truth." When Jesus says that the Spirit
will lead us to the complete truth, he means that
the Spirit will make us full participants in the
divine life, a life that makes us into new people,
living with a new mind and in a new time: the
mind and time of Jesus Christ.

In and through the Spirit of Christ, we
become others' Christs living in all places and at
all times. In and through the Spirit, we come to
know all that Jesus knew, and we are able to do all

that he did. This is the great wisdom of God, the wisdom that none of the masters of this age has ever known, the wisdom which has remained hidden from the learned and the clever but has been revealed to mere children, the wisdom which comes to us through the Spirit and can only be taught to us spiritually.

Thus, discipleship is the life of the Spirit in us, by whom we are lifted up into the divine life itself and receive new eyes to see, new ears to hear, and new hands to touch. Being lifted up in God's own life, we are sent into the world to witness to what we have seen with our own eyes, have heard with our own ears, and have touched with our own hands. It is a witness to the life of God's word in us.

The way of the cross, the downward mobility of God, becomes our way not because we try to imitate Jesus, but because we are transformed into living Christs by our relationship with his Spirit. The spiritual life is the life of the Spirit of Christ in us, a life that sets us free to be strong while weak, to be free while captive, to be joyful while in pain, to be rich while poor, to be on the downward way of salvation while living in the midst of an upwardly mobile society.

Although this spiritual life may well seem enigmatic, intangible, and elusive to us who live in a scientific age, its fruits leave little doubt about the radical transformation it brings about. Love, joy, peace, patience, kindness, goodness, trustfulness, gentleness, and self-control are indeed the qualities of our Lord himself and reveal his presence in the midst of a world so torn apart by idolatry, envy, greed, sexual irresponsibility, war, and other sin (see Galatians 5:19–23). It is not hard to distinguish the upward pull of our world from the downward pull of Christ.

44

2.

TEMPTATION

The Lure of Upward Mobility

The spiritual life is the life of the Spirit of Christ within and among us. The Holy Spirit leads us on the downward way, not to cause us to suffer or to subject us to pain and humiliation, but rather to help us to see God present in the midst of our struggles. Just as we came to see God in the downward way of Christ, so we will become conscious of truly being sons and daughters of God by becoming participants in this downward way, the way of the cross.

The gospels depict Jesus on the eve of his death making clear to his disciples that their ministry is possible only because they no longer belong to the world and its ways. In his priestly prayer to his Father, he says, "They do not belong to the world any more than I belong to the world." It is this not-belonging that is the basis for their mission: "I am not asking you to remove them from the world, but to protect them from the Evil One . . . As you sent me into the world, I have sent them into the world" (John 17:15–19). In these words, Jesus tells us that the Spirit by whom we participate in the divine life is the same Spirit who allows us to be in the world without being of it.

The world, however, is the place where the Evil One roams. It is the home of the tempter who wants to snatch us away from God and return us to the road of upward mobility. We must face and deal with this tempter eye to eye. As Jesus was sent by the Spirit into the desert to be tempted, so are we. It may be that the true quality of the spiritual life can only be recognized in the face of our temptations.

Three temptations by which we are confronted again and again are the temptation to be relevant, the temptation to be spectacular, and the temptation to be powerful. All three are temptations to return to the ways of the world of upward mobility and divert us from our mission to reveal Christ to the world.

The Temptation to Be Relevant

The first temptation with which the devil accosted Jesus was that of turning stones into loaves of bread. This is the temptation to be relevant, to do something that is needed and can be appreciated by people—to make productivity the basis of our ministry.

How often have we heard these words: "What is the value of talking about God to hungry people? What is the use of proclaiming the

Good News to people who lack food, shelter, or clothing? What is needed are people who can offer real help and support. Doctors can heal, lawyers can defend, bankers can finance, social workers can restructure. But what can *you* do? What do you have to offer?"

This is the tempter speaking!

This temptation touches us at the center of our identity. In a variety of ways we are made to believe that we are what we produce. This leads to a preoccupation with products, visible results, tangible goods, and progress.

The temptation to be relevant is difficult to shake since it is usually not considered a temptation, but a call. We make ourselves believe that we are called to be productive, successful, and efficient people whose words and actions show that working for God's Reign is at least as dignified an occupation as working for General Electric, Mobil Oil, or the government. But this is giving in to the temptation to be relevant and respectable in the eyes of the world.

When Jesus was tempted to turn stones into bread, he said to the tempter, "One does not live by bread alone, but by every word that comes from the mouth of God." Jesus did not deny the importance of bread but rather relativized it in comparison with the nurturing power of the Word of God. In the book of Deuteronomy, Moses says to his people, "Yahweh made you feel hungry and fed you with manna which neither you nor your fathers had known, to make you understand that people do not live on bread alone but on everything that comes from the mouth of Yahweh" (Deuteronomy 8:3).

Bread is given to us by God so that we will entrust ourselves completely to God's word. Accomplishments, efficiency, and productivity are gifts that can be given to those whose hearts are fixed on the Lord first. What this says is not that relevant behavior needs to be despised, but that it should not be the basis for our identity as Christians.

We are not the bread we offer, but people who are fed by the Word of God and thereby find true selfhood. The radical challenge is to let God and the divine Word shape and reshape us as human beings, to feast each day on this Word and thus grow into free and fearless people. Thus we can continue to witness to God's presence in this world, even when there are few or no visible results.

To be a Christian who is willing to travel with Christ on his downward road requires being willing to detach oneself constantly from any need to be relevant, and to trust ever more deeply the Word of God. Thus, we do not resist the temptation to be relevant by doing irrelevant things but by clinging to the Word of God who is the source of all relevancy.

The Temptation to Be Spectacular

The second temptation which Jesus faced and which we face as well is the temptation to be spectacular. The devil took Jesus to the holy city, made him stand on the parapet of the temple, and said, "If you are the Son of God, throw yourself down; for the scripture says: 'He will put you in his angels' charge, and they will support you on their hands in case you hurt your foot against a stone'" (Matthew 4:5–6). It is the temptation to force God to respond to the unusual, the sensational, the extraordinary, the unheard of—and then to force people to believe.

The temptation to do something spectacular has not lessened since Jesus' day. We have come to believe that a service is valuable when many attend, a protest or demonstration is worthwhile when television cameras are present, a study group is worth having when many want to be part of it, and a church is successful when many desire to become members. "Truth" in our culture has become so largely determined by statistics that it is easy for us to truly believe that the number of people who listen, watch, or attend is a measure of the quality of that which is presented.

It is difficult for us to believe that salvation came from the remnant of Israel. It is difficult for us to believe that something very good came from an unknown place. It is difficult for us to believe that our God is a God who came in the unspectacular form of a servant, who entered Jerusalem on an ass, and who was killed as a common criminal.

And it is even more difficult to believe that a few unsophisticated fishermen brought God's good news to the world.

We act as if visibility and notoriety were the main criteria of the value of what we are doing. It is not easy to act otherwise. Statistics do rule our society. The biggest box-office hits, the best-selling books, the fastest-selling cars, the record-breaking athletes—these are the signs that we are dealing with something significant. To be spectacular is so much our concern that we, who have been spectators most of our lives, can hardly conceive that what is unknown, unspectacular, and hidden can have any value.

How do we overcome this all-pervading temptation? It is important to realize that our hunger for the spectacular—like our desire to be relevant—has very much to do with our search for selfhood. To be a person and to be seen, praised, liked, and accepted have become nearly the same for many. Who am I when nobody pays attention, says thanks, or recognizes my work? The more insecure, doubtful, and lonely we are, the greater our need for popularity and praise.

Sadly, this hunger is never satisfied. The more praise we receive, the more we desire. The hunger for human acceptance is like a bottomless barrel. It can never be filled.

Jesus responded to the tempter, "You must not put the Lord your God to the test." Indeed, the search for spectacular glitter is an expression of doubt in God's complete and unconditional acceptance of us. It is indeed putting God to the test. It is saying: "I am not sure that you really care, that you really love me, that you really consider me worthwhile. I will give you a chance to show it by soothing my inner fears with human praise and by alleviating my sense of worthlessness by human applause."

Our true challenge is to return to the center, to the heart, and to find there the gentle voice that speaks to us and affirms us in a way no human voice ever could. The basis of all ministry is the experience of God's unlimited and unlimiting acceptance of us as beloved children, an acceptance so full, so total, and all-embracing, that it sets us free from our compulsion to be seen, praised, and admired and frees us for Christ, who leads us on the road of service.

This experience of God's acceptance frees us from our needy self and thus creates new space where we can pay selfless attention to others. This new freedom in Christ allows us to move in the world uninhibited by our compulsions and to act creatively even when we are laughed at and reject-ed, even when our words and actions lead us to death. Through a disciplined life of contemplative prayer we slowly can come to realize God's original love, the love that existed long before we could love ourselves or receive any other human love. The apostle John says: "Love comes from God . . . because God is love. We are to love, then, because God loved us first" (1 John 4:7–8, 19).

Contemplative prayer leads us to that first love, the love by which we receive our true self. We are not the votes we receive, but rather we are who God has made us in love: children of the light, children of God. Only a life of ongoing intimate communion with God can reveal to us our true selfhood; only such a life can set us free to act according to the truth, and not according to our need for the spectacular.

This is far from easy. A serious and persevering discipline of solitude, silence, and prayer is demanded. Such a discipline will not reward us with the outer glitter of success, but with the inner light which enlightens our whole being, and which allows us to be free and uninhibited witnesses of God's presence in our lives.

The Temptation to Be Powerful

The third and most seductive temptation to which Jesus was subjected is the temptation to be powerful. The devil showed Jesus all the kingdoms and their splendor and said, "I will give you all these, if you fall at my feet and worship me" (Matthew 4:8–9).

There is probably no culture in which people are so unabashedly encouraged to seek power as ours. From the moment we set out on our climb to the top we make ourselves believe that striving for power and wanting to be of service are, for all practical purposes, the same thing. This fallacy is so deeply ingrained in our whole way of living that we do not hesitate to strive for influential positions in the conviction that we do so for the good of the Reign of God.

It seems nearly impossible for us to believe that any good can come from powerlessness. In this country of pioneers and self-made people, in which ambition is praised from the first moment we enter school until we enter the competitive world of free enterprise, we cannot imagine that any good can come from giving up power or not even desiring it. The all-pervasive conviction in our society is that power is a good and that those possessing it can only desire more of it.

Power can take many forms: money, connections, fame, intellectual ability, skills. These are all ways to get some sense of security and control, and strengthen the illusion that life is ours to dispose of. It is therefore quite understandable that on the personal, as well as on the national and international level, power is the name of the game.

There is almost nothing more difficult to overcome than our desire for power. Power always lusts after greater power precisely because it is an illusion. Despite our experience that power does not give us the sense of security we desire, but instead reveals our own weaknesses and limitations, we continue to make ourselves believe that more power will eventually fulfill our needs.

The result is a spiral of increasing desire for power which parallels a spiral of increasing feelings of weakness. The escalating arms race is one of the more dramatic examples. The more weapons we have, the less freedom we have to move. Thus our country has become musclebound. It looks and behaves like a bodybuilder who has developed his muscles to such a degree that he can no longer move.

Surrounded by so much power, it is very difficult to avoid surrendering to the temptation to seek power like everyone else. But the mystery of our ministry is that we are called to serve not with our power but with our powerlessness. It is through powerlessness that we can enter into solidarity with our fellow human beings, form a community with the weak, and thus reveal the healing, guiding, and sustaining mercy of God. We are called to speak to people not where they have it together but where they are aware of their pain, not where they are in control but where they are trembling and insecure, not where they are self-assured and assertive but where they dare to doubt and raise hard questions; in short, not where they live in the illusion of immortality but where they are ready to face their broken, mortal, and fragile humanity. As followers of Christ, we are sent into the world naked, vulnerable, and weak, and thus we can reach our fellow human beings in their pain and agony and reveal to them the power of God's love and empower them with the power of God's Spirit.

Jesus responded to the temptation of power with the words, "You must worship the Lord your God and serve God alone." These words remind us that only undivided attention to God can make a powerless ministry possible. As long as we divide our time and energy between God and others, we forget that service outside of God becomes self-seeking, and self-seeking service leads to manipulation, and manipulation to power games, and power games to violence, and violence to destruction—even when it falls under the name of ministry.

The true challenge is to make service to our neighbor the manifestation and celebration of our total and undivided service to God. Only when all of our service finds its source and goal in God can we be free from the desire for power and proceed to serve our neighbors for their sake and not our own.

This is the great mystery of servanthood. It is expressed by Jesus when he said to his disciples, "I shall not call you servants any more, because a servant does not know his master's business. I call you friends because I have made known to you everything I have learned from my father" (John 15:15). Here we see that servanthood and friendship are no longer distinct and that in serving God we find our true self which no longer needs social affirmations but is free to offer a powerless ministry.

The temptations of being relevant, spectacular, and powerful are real temptations and stay with us all of our lives. They are strong because they play directly on our desire to join others on the upwardly mobile road.

But when we are able to recognize these temptations as seductive attempts to cling to the illusions of the false self, they can become instead invitations to claim our true self, which is hidden in God alone. When we find ourselves able to continue to serve our fellow human beings even when our lives remain the same, even when few people offer us praise, and even when we have little or no power, we come to know ourselves as God knows us, as sons and daughters hidden in God's love.

We do not belong to the world. We belong to God. We always will be tempted in one way or another to reclaim the old self, to return to Egypt, and to reject the foolish way of the cross. But we become true followers of Jesus Christ each time we take his words on our lips and say to the tempter, "Be off, Satan . . . you must worship the Lord your God and serve him alone."

3.

A Self-Emptied Heart
The Disciplines of Spiritual Formation

Our vocation as Christians is to follow Jesus on his downward path and to become witnesses to God's compassion in the concrete situation of our time and place. Our temptation is to let needs for success, visibility, and influence dominate our thoughts, words, and actions to such an extent that we are gripped in the destructive spiral of upward mobility and thus lose our vocation. It is this life-long tension between vocation and temptation that presents us with the necessity of spiritual formation. Precisely because the downward mobility of the way of the cross cannot rely on our spontaneous responses, we are faced with the question, "How do we conform our minds and hearts to the mind and heart of the self-emptying Christ?"

To follow Christ requires the willingness and determination to let God's Spirit pervade all the corners of our minds and hearts and there make us into other Christs. Formation is transformation, and transformation means a growing conformity to the mind of Christ, who did not cling to his equality with God but emptied himself.

Thus discipleship cannot be realized without discipline. Discipline in the spiritual life, however, has nothing to do with the discipline of athletics, academic study, or job training, in which physical fitness is achieved, new knowledge is acquired, or a new skill is mastered. The discipline of the Christian disciple is not to master anything, but rather to be mastered by the Spirit. True Christian discipline is the human effort to create the space in which the Spirit of Christ can transform us into his lineage.

I would like to call attention to three disciplines by which spiritual formation can take place. They are the discipline of the church, the discipline of the Book, and the discipline of the heart.

The Discipline of the Church

The discipline of the church is the discipline by which we remain in touch with the true story of God in history. One way of defining the spiritual life is to see it as a life in which we keep making connections between God's story and our own.

Without the Spirit, our upwardly mobile lives remain full but unfulfilled lives in which our many stories compete with each other for attention. Without the Spirit, our busy lives remain boring lives in which the many events of each day remain a series of random incidents and accidents. Without the Spirit, our lives remain truly unevent-

ful. But with the Spirit, all that takes place from day to day, week to week, and year to year, can be known and experienced as the concrete manifestations of the Christ-event in time and space.

The discipline of the church is the discipline by which we as a people represent the living Christ in time and space. This living Christ is not simply a person, but an event. Christ is the one who was born, lived, died, rose from the dead, and sent the Spirit. Christ is God acting in human history. It is this mystery of the Christ-event that is made visible in the liturgical discipline of the church.

The liturgy is the celebration by the people of God of the Christ-event. It is the manifestation of what is really taking place in human history. Christ is coming and being born in us; he lives, suffers, dies, and is risen in us; and he sends his Spirit to us, thereby bringing us into communion with one another. The seasonal celebrations of

Christmas, Easter, and Pentecost, and their periods of preparation and reflection, manifest the fullness of the Christ-event of which we have become part.

The first and most essential discipline by which our spiritual formation takes place is, therefore, the discipline by which we, the people of God, create space in the midst of our human chronologies to present the Christ-event as true for us. Thus the church is our first and foremost spiritual director. The church not only teaches us what to reflect on, what to pay attention to, and what to speak or think about, it also realizes in and through the liturgical discipline the Christ-event itself.

What is truly taking place in our lives is not determined by the random ups and downs of our personal and communal lives, but rather by the events of Christ's life being realized among us in and through the church. It is Advent, Christ is coming; it is Christmas, Christ is being born; it is Lent, Christ is suffering; it is Holy Week, Christ is dying; it is Easter, Christ is risen; it is Pentecost, Christ is sending his Spirit. That is what is truly happening! All other events—personal, social, or political—derive their meaning from the Christ-event.

Just as we only come to know our true selves by letting ourselves be known in and through Christ, so, too, can we only come to know the true events of our time in and through the Christ-event. Our true story reveals itself through the story of Christ.

The story of Christ is therefore not "the greatest story ever told," but the only story ever told. It is the story from which all other stories receive their meaning and significance. The story of Christ makes history real.

The attention to the presence of Christ in our own personal story can only remain free from self-deception when we remain attentive to the presence of Christ in the daily life of the church. Only when we allow the total Christ-event as it was prepared in the Old Testament, realized in the New Testament, and proclaimed in the life of the Christian community; only when we can let that event become the foundation of our lives can we make connections by which we are healed and given new life.

The Discipline of the Book

The second discipline by which we are con-formed to the self-emptying Christ is the discipline of the Book. Reading the Scriptures is essential for anyone who wants to follow Christ on the road of downward mobility. Although the church presents us with God's Word each day, we also need to listen to that Word in the intimacy of our own home and let it speak to the most hidden corners of our being.

Christ is the Word of God who became flesh for us. Through the discipline of the Book, the Word of God can continue to become flesh in us. Reading the Scriptures as God's most intimate word for us is thus the realization of the incarnation in the concrete reality of our present life.

This is a real discipline because, when we read the Scriptures, we too often read them merely to be informed or to be instructed, to be edified or to be inspired, or—what is not infrequent—to find a quote to support our own ideas. The Holy Book becomes a book among other books, and is often used in merely that way, just as Jesus became a human being among other human beings, and is often treated merely in that way.

But as Jesus is also the Son of God, so the Holy Scriptures are also the Word of God. By the Word of God we are formed into living Christs, and this formation goes far beyond information, instruction, edification, or inspiration. This formation requires eating the Word, chewing on it, digesting it, and thus letting it become true nourishment. Thus the Word descends from our minds into our hearts and there finds a dwelling place.

This is what meditation is all about. It is the discipline of inner attentiveness to the Word. Among the many texts the church presents to us each year, there might be one word, one story, one parable, one sentence that has the power to turn us around, to change our whole life, to give us a new heart and new mind, to conform us to Christ.

Meditation thus is much more than thinking about the words of Scripture, much more than try-

ing to understand the parables, or analyzing complicated sayings. Meditation is the growing inner availability to the word so that the Word can guide us, can open us, can remove our fears, and come to dwell in us. True meditation is thus letting the Word become flesh in us.

It is through this incarnation of the Word in us that we enter eternal life. "Heaven and earth will pass away," Jesus says, "but my words will never pass away." Jesus is the Word, and his words are everlasting life. His Word is the bread that takes our hunger away, the light that dispels our darkness, and the life that allows us to face death without fear.

I am not talking figuratively. I am not simply saying that the Word is like bread, light, or life. No, reading the Word as a word of God for us is a sacramental event, an event by which the Word becomes present and transforms us into itself.

Only when we see the sacramental quality of the Word can we fully understand the meaning of meditation.

This has concrete implications for our daily lives. It shows us the true meaning of reading and studying. Just as there is only one story from which all other stories receive their meaning, there is only one book from which all other books receive their significance. Thus the reading of Scripture should be the basis of all other types of reading. All our reading—whether devotional, academic, or recreational—should always remain intimately connected with the creative and recreative Word of God. For those who live from every word that comes from the mouth of God, there is no secular literature.

Surrounded by so many books, we have moved far from the discipline of the Book. Reading and studying are often part of our attempts to be more relevant, spectacular, and powerful. Even the reading of Scripture itself can become dangerous for our spiritual life. Many discussions about the Word of God do not bring us closer to God and thus have become tools of Satan. As you well know, Satan also quotes the Bible, and knows quite well how to use it to put us back on the wide road that leads to perdition (Matthew 7:13).

The Discipline of the Heart

The third discipline, which leads us on the way of true discipleship and protects us against the temptations of upward mobility, is the discipline of the heart. The discipline of the heart is the discipline of personal prayer. In the context of the liturgical life of the church, and supported by an ongoing meditation on the Word of God, personal prayer leads us not just to our own heart, but to the heart of God.

The discipline of the heart is probably the discipline we give up most easily. Entering into the solitude of our closet and standing there in the presence of our God with nothing but our own nakedness, vulnerability, and sinfulness, requires an intense commitment to the spiritual life. Personal prayer is not rewarded by acclaim, does not translate into helpful projects, and only rarely leads to the inner experience of peace and joy. Yet, personal prayer is the true test of our vocation.

For us born activists, the discipline of the heart through which we strip ourselves of all scaffoldings and cry out in our misery to the God of mercy and compassion is a discipline of purification. If we indeed desire to see God in and

through the humiliated Christ living among us, and if we indeed want to follow Christ wherever he leads us, we need a pure heart, a heart free from the "oughts" and "musts" of our world.

Jesus says, "When you pray, do not imitate the hypocrites: they love to say their prayers standing up in synagogues and at street corners for people to see them. I tell you solemnly, they have had their reward. But when you pray go to your private room and when you have shut your door pray to your Father who is in that secret place, and your Father who sees all that is done in secret will reward you" (Matthew 6:1–4). To truly become men and women whose identities are hidden in God, we need to have the courage to enter empty-handed into the place of solitude.

There is nothing romantic about this. If we take the discipline of the heart seriously, we have to start by setting aside a time and a place when and where we can be with God and God alone, not once in a while, but regularly. We need to look at our agenda and reserve time for personal prayer so that we can say honestly and without hesitation to those who want to see us at that time, "I am sorry, but I have already made an appointment then and it cannot be changed."

For most of us it is very hard to spend a useless hour with God. It is hard precisely because by facing God alone we are also facing our own inner chaos. We come in direct confrontation with our restlessness, anxieties, resentments, unresolved tensions, hidden animosities, and long-standing frustrations. Our spontaneous reaction to all this is to run away and get busy again, so that we can at least make ourselves believe that things are not as bad as they seem in our solitude.

The truth is that things are bad, even worse than they seem. It is this painful stripping away of the old self, this falling away from all our old support systems that enables us to cry out for the unconditional mercy of God. When we do not run away in fear, but patiently stay with our struggles, the outer space of solitude gradually becomes an inner space, a space in our heart where we come to know the presence of the Spirit who has already been given to us. In the solitude of our heart we can listen to our questions and—as the German poet Rilke says so beautifully—gradually grow, without even noticing it, into the answer.

The discipline of the heart is the discipline by which we create that inner space in which the Spirit of God can cry out in us "Abba Father" (see Romans 8:15). Thus, through the discipline of the heart, we reach the heart of God. When we come to hear the heartbeat of God in the intimacy of our prayer, we realize that God's heart embraces all the sufferings of the world. We come to see that through Jesus Christ these burdens have become a light burden which we are invited to carry.

Prayer always leads us to the heart of God and the heart of the human struggle at the same

time. It is in the heart of God that we come to understand the true nature of human suffering and come to know our mission to alleviate this suffering, not in our own name, but in the name of the one who suffered and through his suffering overcame all evil.

The discipline of the heart has its own special difficulties. There is the temptation to start hoping for personal revelations and sensations. There is the problem of not knowing if we hear God or just our own restlessness. There is the question of how to discern the direction in which the Spirit moves us. But before and above all these special difficulties, there is the simple difficulty of being faithful to the discipline itself. All this suggests that it might be a great help to have a personal spiritual director, especially when we are just starting to take our spiritual life seriously.

A spiritual director is a fellow Christian to whom we choose to be accountable for the discipline of our heart and from whom we may expect a firm commitment to pray for us. The simple fact that we have to reveal to another Christian with some regularity the status of our personal prayer life and the simple knowledge that he or she is lifting us up to God with great love and care, can make all the difference in our spiritual development.

With someone on our side who keeps encouraging us to enter more deeply through our own heart into the heart of God, we will also be freer to be with others in their pain and to discover with them the presence of the healing God in our midst. Thus, the discipline of the heart leads us on the path of compassion; that is, the downward path, which is the narrow road that leads to life (see Matthew 7:13).

CONCLUSION

Vocation, temptation, and formation have been the three core words in these reflections on the intimate relationship between ministry and the spiritual life. We are called to follow Christ on the downwardly mobile road, tempted to choose the broad path of success, fame, and influence, and challenged to subject ourselves to spiritual disciplines in order to gradually conform ourselves to the image of our Lord Jesus Christ.

Vocation, temptation, and formation are life-long challenges. We are called not once, but day in and day out, and we will never know for sure where we are being led. We are tempted at every moment of our day and night and we will never know precisely where our demons will appear.

This lifelong tension between vocation and temptation opens up for us the difficult but promising task of listening to the church, the Book, and our hearts, thus discovering the real presence of God's Spirit within and among us.

We will never be without struggle. But when we persevere with hope, courage, and confidence, we will come to fully realize in our innermost being that through the downward road of Christ we will enter with him into his glory. So let us be grateful for our vocation, resist our temptation, and be ever committed to a life of ongoing formation.

List of Drawings
Vincent Van Gogh
All (except pp. 67 and 84) used with permission of the
Van Gogh Museum, Amsterdam

95